D1317420

Robots Underwater

Richard and Louise Spilsbury

Gareth Stevens
PUBLISHING

ST. JOHN THE BAPTIST PARISH LIBRARY
2920 NEW HIGHWAY 51
LAPLACE, LOUISIANA 70068

Please visit our website, **www.garethstevens.com**.
For a free color catalog of all our high-quality books,
call toll free 1-800-542-2595 or fax 1-877-542-2596.

Library of Congress Cataloging-in-Publication Data

Spilsbury, Richard.
Robots underwater / by Richard and Louise Spilsbury.
p. cm. — (Amazing robots)
Includes index.
ISBN 978-1-4824-3021-9 (pbk.)
ISBN 978-1-4824-3024-0 (6 pack)
ISBN 978-1-4824-3022-6 (library binding)
1. Remote submersibles — Juvenile literature. I. Spilsbury, Richard, 1963-.
II. Spilsbury, Louise. III. Title.
V857.S65 2016
623.8—d23

First Edition

Published in 2016 by
Gareth Stevens Publishing
111 East 14th Street, Suite 349
New York, NY 10003

© 2016 Gareth Stevens Publishing

Produced for Gareth Stevens by Calcium
Editors for Calcium: Sarah Eason and Jennifer Sanderson
Designers: Paul Myerscough and Simon Borrough
Picture researcher: Susannah Jayes

Photo credits: Cover: NOAA; Inside: Corbis: Bettman 39; Dreamstime: Martin Brayley 36, Steirus 30;
Flickr: Hidden Ocean 2005 Expedition: NOAA Office of Ocean Exploration/Jeremy Potter 7, Hidden
Ocean Expedition 2005/NOAA/OAR/OER 11; Forum Energy Technologies (UK) Ltd: 31, 33; Courtesy
Kongsberg Maritime: 8–9, 9 (right); NOAA: Institute for Exploration/University of Rhode Island
15, Terry Kerby/Hawaii Undersea Research Laboratory 14, NOAA Okeanos Explorer Program, 2013
Northeast U.S. Canyons Expedition 17, Nuytco Research Limited 5b, Image courtesy of Mark Spear,
Woods Hole Oceanographic Institution 12–13; Shutterstock: Blvdone 28, Nickolay Khoroshkov 29,
PixOne 42, V Schlichting 34, Shvak 20; U.S. Navy: Journalist 1st Class Jason E. Miller 43; VideoRay
LLC: 1, 24–25, 25r, 35, 37; Wikimedia Commons: Bgregson 44, Myrabella 12r, Rvongher 41, Ed
Schipul 27, U.S. Coastguard 26, U.S. Navy/Petty Officer 2nd Class Jayme Pastoric, U.S. Navy 5t, Frank
van Mierlo: 22, Yannlepage 16; Woods Hole Oceanographic Institution: 19.

All rights reserved. No part of this book may be reproduced in any
form without permission from the publisher, except by reviewer.

Printed in the United States of America
CPSIA compliance information: Batch #CS15GS: For further information contact Gareth Stevens, New York, New York at 1-800-542-2595.

Contents

Chapter 1

Robots at Sea

Around 70 percent of our planet is covered with water, and most of it is the seawater that makes up the world's oceans. Oceans supply valuable resources, from fish to minerals, but through history, countless shipwrecks remind us that these oceans are treacherous places. Humans venture underwater for many reasons, including finding more resources and exploring under the sea. Amazingly, just 5 percent of the oceans have been explored.

In the deepest ocean, the water pressure on a person would be equivalent to them supporting 50 jumbo jets!

Risky Business

Exploring underwater is a risky business for people and there are several problems to be tackled when humans go underwater for any length of time. They need air to breathe, suits or another covering to keep them from freezing in the water, and lights because it gets darker the deeper they go. Then there is the additional problem of water pressure. As people go deeper under the water, the weight of the water pushing down on them or their vehicle from above becomes greater. This pushing force is called water pressure. Without protective walls that can withstand the high pressure of the deep sea, the pressure could crush a person's lungs.

When humans come up from the deep ocean they go into a decompression chamber to adjust to normal air pressure.

Even traveling underwater in a submersible is still dangerous. It is much safer to send down robots to explore the deep ocean.

The First ROVs

Undersea operations are a great application for robotics to replace humans. Over the years, there have been many different robotic devices but in 1953, Dimitri Rebikoff developed the first remotely operated vehicle (ROV). The ROV, called *POODLE*, was the first really useful underwater robotic device. *POODLE* allows the vehicle's operator to remain in a comfortable environment, while the ROV works in the hazardous environment below. In the 1960s, the US Navy funded most of the early ROV technology development in its quest to develop robots that could perform deep-sea rescue operations and recover objects from the ocean floor, such as nuclear bombs.

Remotely Operated Vehicles

Today there is a huge range of ROVs, from small versions the size of a microwave oven to heavyweights as large a small van. These ROVs are different sizes so they can perform different tasks. Small ROVs can access tiny spaces and large ones can carry a lot of equipment.

The Umbilical

All ROVs have one thing in common: they are connected to a ship by an umbilical. The umbilical is a group of cables that supplies power to the ROV so that it can work, and so that video and data signals can travel back and forth between the ROV and an operator on the ship. Without an umbilical, the ROV would not work.

Some ROVs can work at depths of thousands of feet. Very long umbilicals can become tangled around the underwater structures that ROVs are working on. This is why some ROVs are connected to a second craft floating on the surface directly above them. The floating craft is connected to the ship by a heavy-duty floating umbilical and the ROV can move around freely beneath it.

Parts of the ROV

In addition to the umbilical, these are the other parts of a typical ROV:

▶ **Frame:** this is a metal or plastic cage that supports the other parts of the ROV. The frame also helps protect internal parts such as motors, so they do not become damaged if the ROV hits something underwater.

▶ **Floats:** these are either pieces of foam filled with air bubbles or gas-filled tanks. They provide buoyancy for the ROV so that it does not sink.

▶ **Thrusters:** the thrusters are motors that spin propellers or pump out water to push against the surrounding water. These are sometimes fixed in one position and in other cases they rotate to thrust in different directions.

▶ **Camera:** video cameras mounted on the ROV allow operators on the surface to see around the robot and the obstacles it encounters underwater.

▶ **Lights:** lighting up the ROV's surroundings makes filming easier and it also allows operators to control the ROV's tools to perform jobs efficiently.

▶ **Robot arms:** these can stretch around the ROV and can have a variety of tools mounted on their ends to do different work. For example, gripper hands pick up objects and cutters can cut pipes.

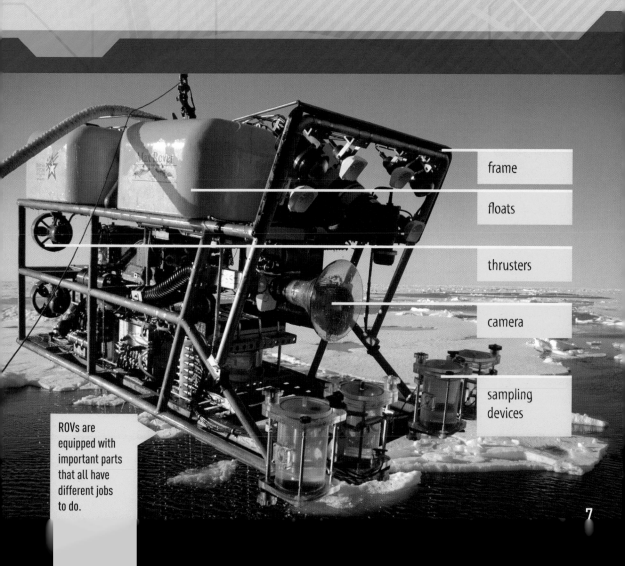

frame

floats

thrusters

camera

sampling devices

ROVs are equipped with important parts that all have different jobs to do.

7

On Their Own

Today, some of the most advanced underwater robots around are autonomous underwater vehicles (AUVs). Unlike ROVs, these vehicles have shed their umbilicals so they are free to roam the oceans without being tethered to a ship. AUVs have batteries inside them, which provide a power supply to operate their thrusters.

Remus is equipped with sensors, navigation tools, and power resources to enable oceanic surveys over large areas.

All Shapes and Sizes

AUVs come in a variety of shapes. Some look like torpedoes, with a single propeller for power at the back of a long barrel-shaped body. Some look like gliders, with long wings and tail fins for stability in the water as they move quickly along. Others have a stubbier shape. *SENTRY* is an AUV designed to explore the deep ocean up to 13,123 feet (4,000 m). *SENTRY*'s shape makes it possible for it to dive to deep levels using its four thrusters, each mounted on a short, pivoting wing. It can move along at up to 3 feet per second (0.9 m per second) and has a battery life of 40 hours. *SENTRY* is used to collect data, including photographs, as well as chemical and depth measurements.

Using Sensors

Many AUVs navigate themselves without constant human control. They have sensors that detect the AUV's speed and they monitor their position in the ocean using underwater acoustic (sound) sources, called beacons. An onboard computer constantly compares the actual distance from the beacon with its programmed route, which contains data about what distance the AUV should be from a fixed network of beacons. Then it can adjust the AUV's thrusters to follow the correct course. Some AUVs can change their own course, for example, if sensors detect changes around them. If a sensor finds large quantities of a chemical in the water, the AUV may change its course to find the source of the chemical. This is useful in locating sources of pollution.

Remus is shaped like a torpedo to help it move quickly and easily through the water.

Robots Are the Future

AUVs of the future will have greater endurance and range, owing to better batteries. They will be able to hover over one spot on the seafloor to take high-definition photographs. They will also operate in high pressure in the deepest parts of the ocean. Improved sensors will allow them to record data faster and in much greater detail than they can now.

Robots in Demand

Underwater robots, be they ROVs or AUVs, are adaptable vehicles. They can be used in a wide range of industries where people need to work, study, or do other activities at depth. Most underwater robots are at work in the oil and natural gas industry. These energy resources are in high demand because companies have to operate in increasingly deep water to access oil and natural gas sources beneath the seafloor.

All in a Day's Work!

ROV workers are also used to lay cables at great depths. A significant amount of the information we access on the Internet travels through data cables stretching across ocean floors. Robots help position and maintain these vital information highways. Robots also inspect many underwater structures, from bridges to the bottom of supertanker hulls. ROVs and AUVs are on hand to study ocean life and seafloor changes, such as volcanoes or earthquakes. They can be used to search for missing airplanes, submarines, or ships, and recover any survivors after these accidents. They can also collect data explaining why accidents happened.

Climate Science

ROVs and AUVs are proving to be vital tools in studying climate change. Most scientists now accept that Earth's climate is changing rapidly, from higher average temperatures in some places to increased storms, as a result of global warming. This is the increase in average global temperature caused by gases trapping heat in the atmosphere, and these gases are mostly released through human activities. Underwater robots help us spot the signs of climate change at sea, such as changing ocean temperatures, melting polar ice, stronger ocean storms, and changing populations of ocean life.

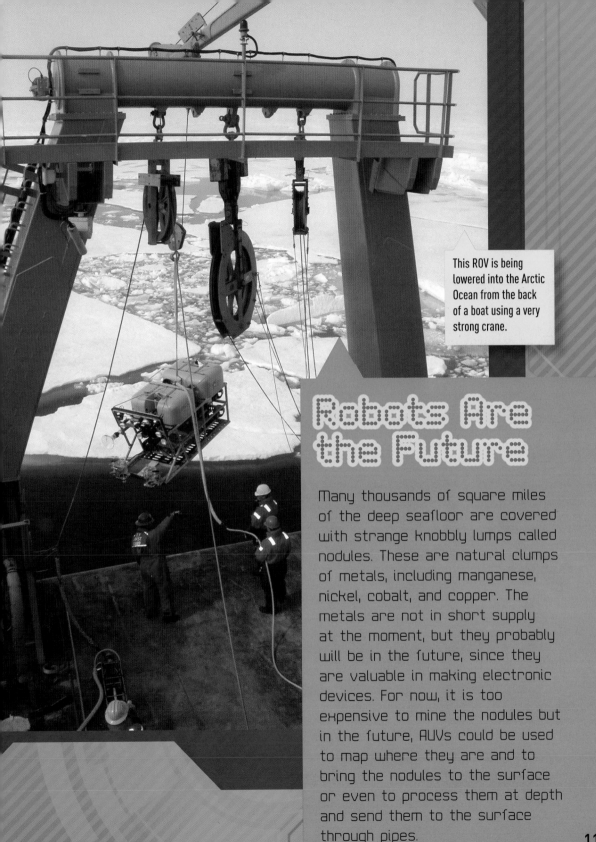

This ROV is being lowered into the Arctic Ocean from the back of a boat using a very strong crane.

Robots Are the Future

Many thousands of square miles of the deep seafloor are covered with strange knobbly lumps called nodules. These are natural clumps of metals, including manganese, nickel, cobalt, and copper. The metals are not in short supply at the moment, but they probably will be in the future, since they are valuable in making electronic devices. For now, it is too expensive to mine the nodules but in the future, AUVs could be used to map where they are and to bring the nodules to the surface or even to process them at depth and send them to the surface through pipes.

11

Chapter 2

Ocean Explorers

When people first started to explore what was underwater, they could dive only as deep as they could go when holding their breath. Later, divers used hollow reeds to breathe through while they swam along looking underwater. They also carried bags of air with them. Gradually inventors came up with more innovative ways of extending a diver's time underwater.

Early Explorers

From very early on people used diving bells to go deep underwater. These were heavy containers made of metal, wood, or glass that sank down and trapped a bubble of air that the diver could breathe inside. In the 1930s, US inventors William Beebe and Otis Barton designed a bathysphere. This was a ball-shaped steel vessel that had round windows for viewing the world underwater. It was lowered by cable from a ship. The bathysphere's first trip took it to 1,312 feet (400 m). Then, between 1946 and 1948, a more maneuverable bathyscaphe was built.

This diving suit was invented in 1882. It was made from steel and glass.

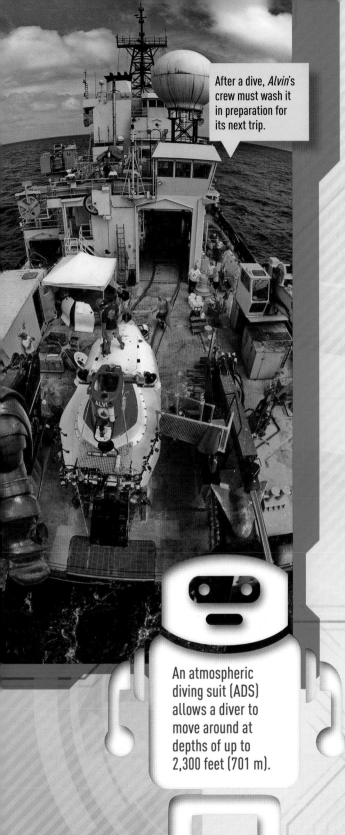

After a dive, *Alvin*'s crew must wash it in preparation for its next trip.

An atmospheric diving suit (ADS) allows a diver to move around at depths of up to 2,300 feet (701 m).

This vehicle had a steel cabin for two passengers and another container filled with gasoline, which is lighter than water, so it acted as a float. Bathyscaphes were the first vehicles to explore the seabed in deep underwater trenches.

Alvin *the Submersible*

Alvin is the world's oldest research submersible. *Alvin* is a human operated vehicle (HOV) with robotic parts. It can carry two passengers and a pilot on dives that last up to 10 hours. It uses thrusters to help it hover in the water, move over rugged seabeds, and rest on the seafloor. Scientists can look at the world around them from small windows and record images on video or still cameras. To light up the dark world deep underwater, *Alvin* is equipped with strong LED lights that can illuminate the seafloor and the space above it. *Alvin* also has two robotic arms that can be used to handle different tools. The arms can pick up around 400 pounds (181 kg) of samples from the seafloor. It places the samples in a basket so that they can be brought to the surface.

Historical Research

Many robot explorers are used for historical research. They dive deep down to find and observe or study shipwrecks, which can tell us interesting historic information. Shipwrecks are like time capsules from the past because they go down with their cargo, clothes, cooking utensils, tools, and much more. They can provide us with evidence about how people lived, how they built their ships, what they used them for, and how they helped to shape the world we know today.

Shipwrecks Close Up

Underwater robots can provide experts with a close look at shipwrecks deep under the sea. They can use sensors, high-definition cameras, and other technology to explore the surface of shipwrecks, but they are also small enough

The submersible *Pisces IV* examines the wreck of a US landing craft from World War II.

This ROV is studying the stern (the rear) of the famous shipwreck of the *Titanic*.

to drive inside many wrecks to view or collect artifacts inside. Exploring shipwrecks is very dangerous for human divers because of the risk of the shipwreck collapsing and trapping or killing them.

Inside the Titanic

The *Titanic* is possibly the most famous of all shipwrecks. The passenger ship, which set sail from the United Kingdom in 1912, sank after hitting an iceberg on its first voyage. Around 1,500 people died. The *Titanic* remained 12,467 feet (3,800 m) at the bottom of the ocean for many years before finally being explored in 1985 by an underwater robot called *Jason Junior*. This ROV had a remote-controlled camera and fed live images of the ship's interior to a monitor.

Robots Are the Future

Colonies of bacteria are growing on the surface of the *Titanic* and eating away at the ship's steel hull. To prevent further decay, there are plans to use underwater robots to clean *Titanic*'s hull and coat it with a layer of protective paint. Cleaning bots like these are already used to clean ships in docks. They could save the ship's hull from splitting open and exposing all its precious contents to salt water and wildlife that would destroy them.

15

Scientific Research

Scientists research deep underwater for many different reasons. Some scientists explore deep oceans to discover creatures that have never been seen or named before. A scientific study of global oceans from 2000 to 2010 found 1,200 new species, and scientists estimate there could be 750,000 more species yet to be found and identified. Scientists also study the temperature of the oceans and levels of pollution or chemicals in the water to help them understand changes to the climate and the effects of human activity on ocean water and wildlife.

Spray gliders move through the ocean like aircraft glide through the air above us.

Good Support

Support ships carry the robots used for underwater research and also the scientists, who know where to send the robots and can tell if they have made a useful discovery. The ships receive the information the robots send up, and they have onboard laboratories that scientists can work in to study any material collected by the robots.

Spray Gliders

Spray gliders are AUVs or robotic submarines that are designed to travel in the ocean, gathering data over long periods of time. They carry a variety of sensors, which they use on a route programmed by researchers at depths of up to 4,921 feet (1,500 m). Spray gliders are used to collect information through different levels of water as they glide down and then up again. The data they collect help scientists understand more about the temperature, salinity (saltiness), and layers of sediments in particular parts of the ocean. Scientists use this information to learn how the oceans affect climates.

Spray gliders are 6.5 feet (2 m) long, with a wingspan of 3.9 feet (1.2 m). They are streamlined in shape to help them move quickly and easily through the water. They move up and down, or rise and float, by pumping oil between two tanks, which adjusts their position by making them denser or lighter than the water around them. The great advantage of these battery-powered AUVs is that because they glide along gently, they do not use much power, so they can stay in the water for much longer than most data-collecting AUVs.

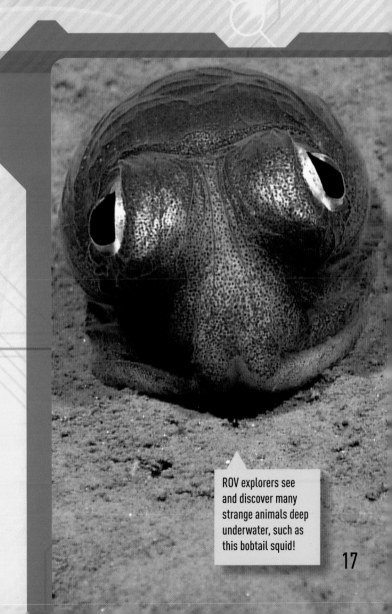

ROV explorers see and discover many strange animals deep underwater, such as this bobtail squid!

17

Underwater robots are being used to help develop maps of the ocean floor. The oceans cover nearly two-thirds of the world's surface and the ocean floor is as varied as the land above its surface, with flat plains, valleys, trenches, and mountains. Measuring the depths of the oceans and mapping the ocean floor helps ships navigate safely. In addition to this, the shape of the seafloor affects ocean currents, and these currents affect the planet's climate. Climate changes can increase the risk of disasters, such as tsunamis, so it is vital to know what is down there.

Underwater Mapping

The AUVs that map the ocean depths and floor are designed to skim along above the changing surface of the ocean floor. Many have two hulls connected by metal bars to help make the vehicles stable so that they do not roll over. They also keep the instruments on board in a steady position as they move along, collecting data. The electronics and batteries are housed in the upper hull and the sensors are contained in the lower hull. The AUVs carry cameras and imaging sonar, which uses the reflected echoes from sounds it emits to build up a picture of what is around it. They also carry sensors for measuring salinity and temperature.

Robots on Ice!

Antarctic scientists are using underwater robots to map the underside of enormous ice floes. In 2014, a yellow *SeaBED* robot, about 6.5 feet (2 m) long sent back the first detailed, 3D maps of Antarctic sea ice. The maps gave scientists accurate measurements of the thickness of ice from areas that were previously too difficult to access. The *SeaBED* took the measurements using an upward-pointing sonar device as it swam

The *SeaBED* has two hulls to help keep it stable so that it can take clear images.

up and down in a grid pattern at a depth of 65 to 98 feet (20 to 30 m). The data it sent back was used to build a 3D map of the underside of the ice. The maps help scientists understand more about the structure of sea ice and the differences between Arctic and Antarctic sea ice.

The Antarctic *SeaBED* explorers can travel at about 14 inches per second (35 cm per second).

Chapter 3

Oil and Gas Workers

Today, ROVs have become an important tool for the oil and natural gas industries. ROVs are used to explore the ocean to find more of these fossil fuels. Vast quantities of oil and natural gas are used around the world. Oil fuels cars, trucks, and other vehicles, and it is used to make plastics and chemicals, pesticides, and many other products. Natural gas is used to generate electricity, for cooking, heating houses, buildings, and water, and for powering factories.

Robots are used to construct and maintain oil rigs. A ship is transporting this rig into the deep ocean.

What Are Fossil Fuels?

Oil and natural gas are formed from the remains of microscopic animals that lived in the sea more than 300 million years ago, and are often under the rock on the seafloor. To get these fossil fuels, large oil platforms, often called oil rigs, are built out at sea. People then drill down into the rock beneath the seafloor to pump up the oil and natural gas buried deep within the floor. There are several stages in the oil and gas industry. First, companies must find oil and gas reserves, or places where there are enough of the fossil fuels to make it worth drilling down to extract them. Then the oil or gas field has to be mapped, test wells drilled, and the drilling rigs brought in. Pipelines and storage facilities must be built, and when the oil and gas platform is working, the fuels need to be shipped to where they are processed.

Using Robots

Robots can be used as a tool in drilling, development, and repairing offshore platforms. They can be used with different manipulators and tools designed for working on equipment in a particular setting. Robots also save human workers from doing incredibly risky jobs. For example, in the past, each time a drill bit wore out, it had to be replaced by a human diver. Attaching a new drill bit to a huge drill that would then drop from above was very dangerous. Today such work is done by ROVs.

Robots Are the Future

In the future, there may be autonomous oil rigs that use GPS coordinates to travel by themselves to a site. They would then build a frame to stand on and drill a well. When this robotic oil rig builder has finished and set up one site, it will be able to pack up and move to the next site, restarting the process.

Construction and Drilling

Building a structure in the ocean is expensive and requires highly trained crews to carry out great feats of engineering. A range of ROVs is used to help crews with the positioning, constructing, and drilling stages of installing an oil platform.

Installing an Oil Platform

The first stage in installing an oil platform is positioning the oil rig. ROVs use onboard equipment, such as video cameras and sonar, to survey the seabed to check the best position for the platform legs. The ROVs can be programmed to follow a preplanned route linked to a 3D simulation of the seafloor,

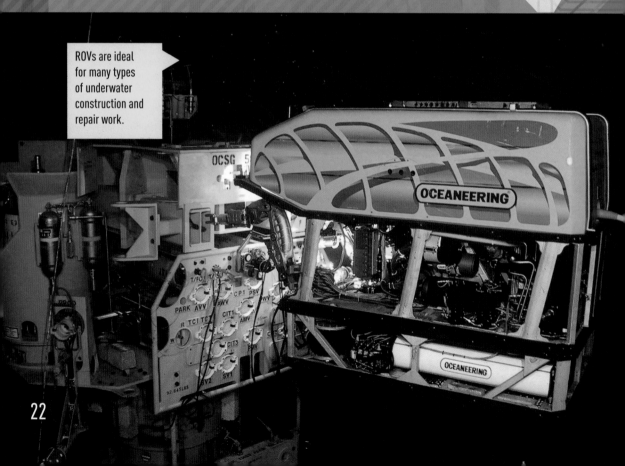

ROVs are ideal for many types of underwater construction and repair work.

which shows the operator exactly where the robot is. They can also be programmed to use their robotic arms to clear debris from the construction site as they move around. In the construction stage of the oil platform, large worker ROVs can be used to put objects into position. The ROV can automatically move into position, with an operator watching over it and changing the plan if required, and once it is in a steady position, it can use its hefty robotic arm to lift parts of the platform frame into position.

ROVs are also used when drilling starts and when pipes are laid to carry the oil and natural gas away. ROVs monitor the movement of the drill and the blowout preventer (BOP). The BOP is a large valve at the top of a well that can be closed if the drilling crew loses control of the oil flow. ROVs also monitor the laying of pipes on a seabed, in order to spot unexpected obstacles and to confirm the pipe is laid correctly before it is too late to recover it.

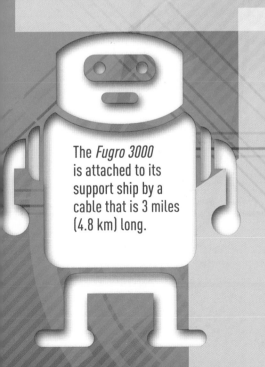

The *Fugro 3000* is attached to its support ship by a cable that is 3 miles (4.8 km) long.

Working-Class Robots

The ROVs are stored on either side of huge support ships, which have cranes that can launch and retrieve them from the water. The largest and heaviest worker ROVs are powered electrically and hydraulically, which is what enables them to do some heavy lifting using a variety of manipulators and grabbers that can be attached to their powerful arms. They can even use power tools and cutters. These big ROVs can work in waters up to 10,000 feet (3,048 m) deep!

Maintenance and Repair

Building platforms and pipes is only part of the ROV's job. Once the structures are in place, they have to be checked and maintained. Oil and natural gas are expensive, and leaks cost money and can damage the ocean environment. They are also flammable and can be dangerous. Making sure that pipes and platforms are maintained keeps the human workers safe. It is usually slower to complete work underwater using robots but it is much safer than using human divers.

ROV Inspectors

Small observation ROVs about the size of a soccer ball are often called "flying eyeballs." They can move around underwater and get close to pipes and platforms in order to inspect them. They are equipped with a digital video inspection system that can display and record footage from several cameras at the same time. They can be programmed to follow the length of a pipe or a leg of a platform to check for cracks and leaks. As well as sending images to screens in ships or on platforms above, ROVs can also use instruments to monitor the effects of rusting on pipes and estimate how much damage is done by the growth of tiny animals and bacteria on the metal pipes and frames.

Observation ROVs like this one are designed to be small so that they can get into tight spaces.

Pipe Support

After laying pipes on the ocean floor, waves can wash away the sand or rock beneath sections of the pipe. This leaves that section of pipe unsupported, which could result in it bending or cracking. When this happens, ROVs are often used to take filled bags down to the correct section of pipe. They slide the bags under various points along the length of the pipeline to support it.

ROVs can have strong gripper arms attached to the front to perform different tasks.

Cleaning Up

When there is a problem, ROVs can also be used to solve it. They can have attachments fitted to remove and scrape away marine growth. They can use manipulators and suction cups to hold onto vertical structures and systems of brushes, water jets, and other abrasive (rubbing) devices to clear those structures off.

Robots Are the Future

RoboTuna is a robot that is designed to swim like a real tuna fish. It is hoped that a design like this might make for a quicker, more energy-efficient underwater robot, which could be used for underwater exploration or inspection in the future.

Oil Emergencies

Oil is a vital resource for the modern age, but it is not without its problems. Every year, trillions of gallons of oil are extracted from the earth and transported to refineries by pipes or tankers. Inevitably accidents happen and oil is spilled by damaged tankers, pipelines, or oil rigs. This oil sticks to everything it touches and can cause terrible and long-lasting damage to oceans and coasts.

When offshore drilling units are damaged, oil can leak into the ocean, causing a lot of damage.

Robot Fixers

Robots are increasingly being used to clean up oil accidents and spills. Underwater robots can be used to dive to great depths and take their time exploring the well site. They can be used to collect video footage and data from sensors that help engineers understand what caused the problem. The information can tell them what they need to do to fix it. ROVs can also be used to fix problems when necessary. ROVs have hydraulic arms with interchangeable tools, such as saws and cutters, which are used for intervention tasks. ROVs can cut off the BOP or cap, or block the top of a well to prevent more oil spilling out. After a well is capped, robots can be used to check that no more oil is escaping from the well.

ROVs can use cutters to cut off BOPs and stop the oil flow.

Robots Are the Future

Oil spills can be extremely difficult to clean up, so scientists have been looking for ways to clean these spills using robots with special filters. The idea is to clean up the oil as quickly as possible from the surface, before it sinks into the ocean floor and causes too much damage. A new Airborne Robotic Oil Spill Recovery System (AEROS) could use special robots that will be lowered from aircraft into the area of an oil spill.

The autonomous robots will then clean oil spills in just a few days by collecting and then spinning oily water to separate the two parts of the mixture. They will then release the water and collect the oil, which can be recycled. The robots can work nonstop, 24 hours a day, until the job is done, and can be controlled remotely from an aircraft or base station via satellite. It is estimated that large oil spills could be cleaned up in just a few days by one of these robots!

Chapter 4

Cable Layers

Every time you access a social media website or listen to new music online, it is likely that you have just used a submarine communications cable! About 97 percent of all global communications move through cables laid on the seafloor to link continents together. Submarine cables are not new—the first was laid in 1850 between the United Kingdom and France. Then they carried telegraph messages, but today's versions carry data. Data are streams of electrical signals representing anything from images and live television, to documents and conversations. There are also submarine cables that carry power. They may connect offshore wind farms or wave power plants with electrical grids on land, taking the electricity that they generate to the people who use it.

Data Cabling

Submarine cables for communications and power are usually laid from big coils on cabling ships. They usually follow straight lines on the seafloor, from deep to shallow locations. Typically, cables are kept separate but sometimes they may be close together or crisscrossed, perhaps at points on the seafloor where there is a narrow channel with

When you make a call over the Internet, it is likely that a robot laid the cables that made it possible!

steep rocks around it. Cables are tough but can be damaged if installed on sharp rocks or in places where they get dragged by strong currents or by human activity. Fishing nets and ship anchors can land on or drag cables. Damaged cables slow the flow of data and interrupt communications. ROVs are important equipment for cable-laying companies because they can be used to help lay cables in the best places and be on hand to repair any damaged cables, regardless of how deep a cable is positioned.

Inside a Cable

Submarine communications cables might be tough, but they are made from glass! They contain fiber optics, which are strands of glass not much thicker than your hair. Data move through these as pulses of light moving up to 186,000 miles (300,000 km) per second! Cables can stretch for hundreds of miles carrying data. The strength in cables comes from steel armor wires, and the wires also contain an insulating and waterproofing outer layer and a copper wire to carry power.

Just one glass fiber can carry 375 million telephone conversations at the same time.

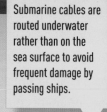

Submarine cables are routed underwater rather than on the sea surface to avoid frequent damage by passing ships.

Cable Positioning

Cabling ships are wide and stable so they are not rocked by waves as they lay cables. They are easy to spot because they usually have an enormous reel of cable on board at the back. They also have large rollers at the back for the cable to roll out over without getting damaged. These ships have sonar systems to survey the shape of the seafloor to determine the best laying route, but the images operators see on board may lack detail. This is when cable layers may use ROVs for a closer inspection. These eyeball ROVs are dispatched to the laying site where they send back video feed of the surroundings and also take more detailed sonar images so that operators can confirm cable positioning routes.

Plows

Some submarine cables are laid using giant towed plows, which cabling ships pull along the seafloor. They dig a trench, automatically lay the cable in it, and then cover it to make it less likely to be damaged by trawler nets and anchors. However, these plows do not work well on slopes and in very fine sediments on the seafloor, because the sediments collapse as the plow digs them. When this happens, ROV trenchers are deployed. These heavy robots

Ships like this one are specifically designed and built to lay cables on the seafloor.

The trenchers that help lay cables are heavy and hard-working ROVs.

are often lowered from cranes on a ship to the seafloor, onto a section of cable that has already been laid. The ROVs have caterpillar treads that raise them above the seafloor so that they can move along the cable without crushing it. These ROVs have pumps to take in water and then blast it out at high pressure. The pumps blow away sediments, leaving a trench up to 10 feet (3 m) deep for the cable. ROVs use arms and other pushing tools to keep the cable safe from the trenching tools and to push it into the trench once it has been dug. They then blow sediments over the top of the cable. By having onboard video feeds, operators on the cabling ship can check that the cable is correctly covered, whatever the type of seafloor. Many ROV trenchers also have thrusters so that they can be used to move underwater to other cable burial sites.

Some ROV trenchers have high-power cutters to cut trenches in rocky seafloors.

Repairing Cables

When cables are damaged hundreds or thousands of feet below the ocean surface, ROVs can help make repairs in conditions where human divers could not easily work. Operators on ships use electrical and optical measurements from the cable to locate the point where the cable is failing.

Fixing the Problem

Once the location of the fault is found, the ROV is launched from the ship and it uses its thrusters to reach the failure point. It places a transponder on the seafloor. The transponder produces pulses of sound that operators can use to mark the location of the fault. Then the ROV gets to work.

Trenchers have complicated work to do, so before they go underwater, they are tested in a pool.

First it must use its pump to blast away the sediments covering the cable. It then uses one of its robot arms tipped with a gripper to lift the damaged cable. A powerful hydraulic cutter within the gripper then severs the cable on one side of the damaged section. The ROV connects a weighted rope from the ship to each cut end, and operators on board bring the cable ends to the surface. They attach a buoy to each end so that if they are dropped, they will not sink again.

The cable with the damaged section is then repaired. Technicians cut out the damaged section and patch in a new piece of the same length. During this process, they clean the wires and fibers in the cable and use special equipment to splice the old and new parts together.

The other end of the main cable is then cleaned up and joined to the mended part. Then the joint is sealed inside a waterproof casing, and the completed cable is tested to check that everything is working properly. A winch is then used to slowly lower the cable into position on the seafloor. The ROV use water jets to bury the section again.

Robots Are the Future

In the future, there could be AUVs shaped like octopuses, with arms that can feel around in the darkness of deep oceans. Scientists in Germany have developed very fine sensors that can be printed onto robot arms and which detect very slight stretching caused by touching raised surfaces. This sense of touch will help them locate and mend submarine cables.

Chapter 5

Underwater Inspectors

Any object that is continually underwater or exposed to seawater is under threat. Think of any jagged cliffs you may have seen along coasts or in pictures. They look like that because the immense power of waves has worn them away. This happens to concrete along coasts, too, whether it is making up a breakwater or the tower of an offshore wind turbine. Any metal structures exposed to seawater risk rusting. This is when iron in steel undergoes a chemical reaction with oxygen in air. Structures rust more easily when there is salt in the water or air.

Robots are used to check the underwater sections of offshore wind farms like this one.

A High Cost

It is very time-consuming, expensive, and often dangerous for human divers to inspect structures underwater. However, this is dwarfed by the costs of failing structures. A collapsing bridge would not only endanger lives, but also cause a break in transportation and communication between areas, affecting businesses. Damaged wind turbines, wave power machines, or other ocean power devices cannot generate the electricity that we increasingly depend on. It makes sense for robots to do some of the inspection work.

The *VideoRay* robot can be operated by game controllers and a laptop computer.

Inspection Tools

ROVs and AUVs are widely used to inspect structures. Cameras are not the only tools they have to help with inspection work. In murky water, sonar systems scan all around the ROV to check the shape of structures around it, so inspectors may be able to notice cracks or other signs of damage. Sometimes damage is trickier to spot using these methods. The *VideoRay* AUV can carry an ultrasonic metal-thickness gauge that uses sound to detect if the metal is thinner or thicker than it should be, as a result of rust. It can also carry a laser, which it fires at structures in order to accurately measure the size and scale of any defects.

Robots Are the Future

In the future, deep-sea pipes could be inspected by AUVs that never come to the surface. *FlatFish* is a lightweight, inexpensive AUV with sensors designed to carry out underwater inspections autonomously. *FlatFish* docks on a seafloor base, where it charges. When sensors on pipes detect flow problems, it goes on inspection trips without any help from human operators.

Spotting Changes

Any structures that are mostly or always underwater need regular inspections to spot changes through time. The inspections could reveal new cracks, rust patches, or growths of any unwanted animals. They may also show how existing faults have become worse.

Animal Dangers

The inspections are also used to determine how much damage sea creatures are causing to marine equipment. For example, zebra mussels are a problem because these tiny, shelled animals grow in huge numbers on surfaces underwater, keeping marine equipment from working or blocking pipes that carry water. Barnacles on ship hulls are another problem because they make a hull rough and less streamlined, so it uses more fuel to travel through the water.

This ROV robot submarine is used by police officers in the fight against crime.

Robot Advantages

There are several advantages to using robots for inspections, whether it is in water pipes, on dam walls, or on hydropower turbines or water pumps. Using robots saves human divers from doing this dangerous job. Robots can be designed to fit inside small, narrow spaces, such as pipes. These robots are small enough for workers to carry in a backpack to where they are needed and are then lowered into the water. The robots record video or still images and transmit them back to the operator.

This *VideoRay Pro3* ROV has strong thrusters, so it can operate even in water with strong currents.

Ballast Tanks

Ships need to stay at the right level in the water so that they remain stable, no matter how much cargo they are carrying. To do this, ocean-going ships pump seawater in and out of their ballast tanks. Salty water can rust steel tanks, so in the past, ships had to be removed from the water and put into dry docks. In the docks, human inspectors could climb inside to check for damage.

Removing ships from the water is not only very expensive and dangerous but it also wastes time that could be used to transport goods. Empty tanks are slippery with seaweed and also full of harmful gases. Today, an ROV can do the inspection work at sea. It grips onto and moves along ribs inside the tanks. It transmits images and data to a computer or tablet screen outside the tank, so human workers can decide what needs to be done.

Robots Are the Future

At the moment, once a robot spots a problem in a ballast tank, repairs are scheduled the next time the ship is in dry dock, but in the future the robot could use a welding laser to perform some types of repair work on its own during the inspection.

Nuclear Safety

Globally, nuclear power is an important energy resource, and in some countries, such as France, it is the major energy source. Nuclear power comes from immense amounts of heat produced during nuclear reactions in nuclear fuel.

Underwater Reaction

In many nuclear reactors, reactions happen underwater because the water absorbs heat and makes it safer. As nuclear fuel reacts, it changes into nuclear waste. This is hazardous to people because it is radioactive and produces invisible rays, or particles, that can make humans sick. Overexposure to radiation can kill people. To minimize the danger, the waste is often stored for long periods underwater in large, deep ponds until it becomes less radioactive. A vital part of stopping the release of radioactivity is to make sure that water tanks and pipes in the reactor are not damaged over time, but even with highly protective clothing, nuclear inspectors are at risk.

MOBOT

One of the earliest land ROVs with robot arms, called MOBOT, was developed in 1960 to handle radioactive materials. Some of its technology was adapted to make the first underwater ROVs, so it is no surprise that ROVs are used in the nuclear industry today. Most nuclear plants use compact ROV eyeballs to inspect their reactors and waste storage underwater for possible leaks. To do this, ROVs have video cameras and sensors that monitor the speed of water movement—faster water flow outside a pipe could mean that there is water escaping from it, possibly contaminating clean water with radioactive water. ROVs may have ultrasonic tools to check whether structures are broken or bent out of shape, which could suggest a possible problem. They also have Geiger counters to measure how radioactive something is.

This early remote-controlled handling machine was designed to work in places that were dangerous for humans, such as nuclear radiation facilities.

Some nuclear power plant ROVs have robot arms equipped with tools to mend broken pipes, clear up radioactive sediments from ponds, and retrieve items from ponds that can be decontaminated elsewhere. There are many pipes and other objects within ponds, so ROVs often operate from floating umbilicals and vessels to avoid getting their cables tangled.

Chapter 6

Ocean Investigators

Robot devices such as ROVs and AUVs may not look like detectives, but they are involved in underwater investigations all over the world. When the underwater environment is being damaged and people want to know who or what is causing it, they send down robot investigators. And when a ship crashes unexpectedly into rocks and sinks, robot investigators can help discover what happened.

Investigating Underwater Impacts

AUVs are used by environmental agencies to study underwater ecosystems and to monitor changes caused by human activity. For example, AUVs map coral reefs in great detail and the impacts on them resulting from trawlers. Trawlers usually drag giant nets over the seafloor in search of fish and these not only churn up sediments, but also damage coral colonies. Coral colonies are vital breeding grounds for fish and other marine animals. AUV data shows that after trawling, the corals recover over time and the data also helps scientists make recommendations about when, or if, fishing might be resumed in damaged areas.

Investigating Accidents

When a ship goes down, robots can help investigate what happened and how best to rescue the ship. In January 2012, the cruise liner *Costa Concordia* hit a rock off the Italian coast. The engine room flooded and the ship capsized, killing 32 people. Operators sent ROVs down to see what happened and saw that the ship was balancing on a rock and in danger of falling, so human workers built supports to keep it from sliding deeper into the sea. ROVs monitored the ship constantly. The ROVs also helped rescue divers look for victims and helped discover several bodies. ROVs were used to keep human divers safe during attempts to save the ship. Operators above water were able to use ROVs to see if there was any danger to divers before they entered an area. The size and portability of the small ROVs made them ideal for the *Concordia* project because it meant they could fit into different spaces and openings on the ship.

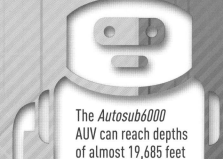

The *Autosub6000* AUV can reach depths of almost 19,685 feet (6,000 m)!

ROVs were used to assess the hull of the *Costa Concordia* shipwreck.

ST. JOHN THE BAPTIST PARISH LIBRARY
2920 NEW HIGHWAY 51
LAPLACE, LOUISIANA 70068

Planes and Subs

In some cases, robotic investigators can also help experts figure out what caused planes and other vehicles to crash and sink. This helps the families of victims come to terms with their loss and can help engineers design safer aircraft and other vehicles in the future.

Using their mechanical arms, ROVS can recover flight recorders from wrecked planes.

Aircraft Investigation

When a French Airbus, on its way from Rio de Janeiro in Brazil to Paris, France, disappeared above a remote part of the Atlantic Ocean in June 2009, killing all 228 people aboard, it took five days to find out where it went down. The Air France plane was found at a depth of about 12,800 feet (3,900 m) but investigators were puzzled as to why it crashed, so plans were immediately made to retrieve the aircraft's black box (flight recorder).

This deep submergence vehicle is used in submarine rescue missions.

Sending in the Remora 2000

An American-built, deep-diving ROV, the *Remora 2000*, is 5 feet (1.5 m) long and can go to a depth of 19,700 feet (6,000 m). This ROV, equipped with two cameras, strong lights, sensors such as scanning sonar, and two manipulators to grasp and move objects, finally retrieved the Air France plane's black box in 2011. The recovery of the black box helped investigators discover that a blockage in some of the aircraft's tubes, combined with the pilots not being trained to handle such a situation, caused the crash.

Submarines on the Seafloor

When a submarine breaks down, gets caught on a cable, or stuck on the seabed, it is vital to get its crew out of the submarine as quickly as possible. ROVs with video and sonar are used to find the precise location of the submarine. Once the submarine has been found, an underwater robot can use its manipulator arm to untangle the vessel if it is caught in a cable or to unblock escape hatches so people can get out. One Russian submarine was in trouble and human rescuers had failed to save it. A remote-controlled robot inspected the netting that was wrapped around the submarine and used strong, pincer-like cutters, designed to slice through thick steel cables, to cut through the net. Once it was free, the crew filled the submarine's ballast tanks with air so that it floated back up to the surface and to safety in just three minutes!

Future Underwater Robots

Robots are already used underwater in many different ways. They are used to explore shipwrecks on the seabed, discover creatures never before seen by human eyes, and construct, check, and repair oil rigs and other offshore structures. They can help solve mysteries about why planes or ships crash and sink, and they can even help rescue people lost at sea. What will underwater robots be used for in the future?

The solar-powered *AUV Tavros* tweets environmental data from oceans.

Diving Deeper

In the future, AUVs will be able to go deeper and be able to show us deep underwater volcanoes and other features that can tell us more about our planet. They will also be able stay underwater, working for much longer and producing much more detailed maps and images. They will probably be used to locate oil and natural gas in even deeper waters, but also help find suitable locations and develop more offshore renewable structures, such as wind farms or tidal water schemes. By checking areas of the seafloor for potential problems, such as landslides, they will be used to help people position fiber-optic cables for telecommunications and seafloor observatories.

Not only will new underwater robots be even better at collecting data, but they will also use different ways to communicate. University of South Florida marine scientists are testing a new underwater robot that can not only analyze what it finds deep underwater, but can also use social media websites such as Twitter to tell people about it! Most underwater robots report wirelessly back to researchers on land, but the solar-powered *Tavros* can compile data and then convert the information into a message that it uploads onto its Twitter account!

Robots Are the Future

In the future, underwater robots could be sent into space to explore oceans there. In 2014, scientists studying images sent back to Earth from space probes discovered an ocean deep under the icy surface of Saturn's tiny moon Enceladus. This ocean could be bigger than the largest of the United States' Great Lakes and scientists think it could support life in the form of microbes. Robots could be sent to see if there is life in space after all.

Glossary

acoustic to do with sound

autonomous able to act on its own, without outside control

AUVs stands for autonomous underwater vehicles, which means they can act on their own once they are programmed

bacteria microscopic living things

blowout preventer (BOP) a large valve at the top of an oil well that can be closed to stop the flow

buoyancy the ability to float

caterpillar treads a metal track that moves around the wheels of a vehicle to help it move across rough ground

climate change a process in which the environment changes to become warmer or colder, drier, or wetter

contaminating making dirty, spoiled, or polluted

currents bodies of water or air moving in a definite direction

denser thicker and heavier

ecosystems communities of living things

fiber optics thin, flexible fibers of glass used to transmit light signals, mainly for telecommunications

fossil fuels fuels formed from the remains of ancient living things

gauge a tool that measures something

Geiger counters devices that detect radioactivity

global warming the increase in the average temperatures across Earth

GPS GPS stands for Global Positioning System, a system of satellites that work together to give people exact locations on Earth

hulls the main bodies of a ship or boat

hydraulic describes machinery that uses the pushing force of liquid under pressure to do work

hydropower the use of moving water to generate electricity

ice floes large sheets of floating ice

insulating protective layer that keeps heat or cold from getting in

laser a very narrow beam of highly concentrated light

minerals solid, naturally occurring substances

navigate to plan or find a route

pesticides substances that kill insects that are considered pests because they damage plants

pollution substances that make water, air, land, or other substances dirty and unsafe to use

pressure pushing force

propellers devices with blades that spin to make a plane or boat move

radioactive when something contains a type of dangerous and powerful energy

rays beams of light

refineries places where unwanted substances in oil are removed

renewable something that can be used again and again. Energy from the sun is renewable because it will not run out

resources materials that are useful

ROVs stands for remotely operated vehicles, which are robots that are tethered to a control ship

salinity saltiness

satellite an electronic device placed in orbit around Earth. Weather satellites are used to collect weather information and communications satellites pass on television and radio signals

sediments tiny pieces of mud, soil, sand, or rock

sensors devices that sense things, such as heat or movement

simulation a 3D computer model of a situation or place

sonar a system that uses sound waves to find and calculate the location, size, and movement of underwater objects

streamlined shaped to help it move easily through air or water

submersible a vehicle that can operate when completely submerged in the water

thrusters engines that move a vehicle or robot by shooting out a jet of fluid in the opposite direction

transponder a device for transmitting and receiving signals

tsunamis long, high sea waves that can cause destruction if they hit a coastline

turbine a device that can be used to generate electricity

ultrasonic sound waves that humans cannot hear

umbilical a cord or cable that attaches one thing to another

For More Information

Books

Ceceri, Kathy, and Sam Carbaugh. *Robotics: Discover the Science and Technology of the Future with 20 Projects* (Build It Yourself). White River Junction, VT: Nomad Press, 2012.

Furstinger, Nancy. *Helper Robots* (Lightning Bolt Books). Minneapolis, MN: Lerner Publications, 2014.

Leider, Rick Allen. *Robots: Explore the World of Robots and How They Work for Us* (The Fact Atlas Series). New York, NY: Sky Pony Press, 2015.

Peppas, Lynn. *Robotics* (Crabtree Chrome). Ontario, Canada: Crabtree Publishing Company, 2014.

Websites

Read more about robotics at:
www.galileo.org/robotics/intro.html

The Monterey Bay Aquarium's website shows you how to build your own ROV at:
www.marinetech.org/main

Discover more about how robots work at:
http://science.howstuffworks.com/robot2.htm

Publisher's note to educators and parents: Our editors have carefully reviewed these websites to ensure that they are suitable for students. Many websites change frequently, however, and we cannot guarantee that a site's future contents will continue to meet our high standards of quality and educational value. Be advised that students should be closely supervised whenever they access the Internet.

Index